Tanisha Owens Barrett

SELL IT LIKE IT'S HOT:

SELL YOUR HOME IN ANY MARKET!

Disclaimer:

The information provided in this book is intended to assist home sellers in optimizing their chances of selling their homes quickly. However, it is important to note that the real estate market is dynamic and subject to various factors beyond the control of the author, publisher, or any individuals associated with this book.

The strategies, tips, and techniques outlined in this book are based on general principles and experiences that have proven effective in certain circumstances. However, they may not guarantee the same results for every home seller or in every real estate market.

The content of this book is for informational purposes only and should not be considered legal, financial, or professional advice. It is always recommended that readers consult with qualified professionals, such as real estate agents, lawyers, or financial advisors, before making any decisions related to selling their homes.

The author and publisher disclaim any responsibility for any loss or liability incurred by readers or third parties as a result of applying the information provided in this book. Home sellers are encouraged to exercise their own judgment and due diligence when implementing the strategies discussed.

By reading this book, you acknowledge and agree that the author and publisher are not responsible for any direct or indirect consequences, losses, or damages arising from the use of the information contained within.

Copyright © 2023 by Tanisha Owens Barrett

All rights reserved. No part of this book may be reproduced in any form on by an electronic or mechanical means, including information storage and retrieval systems, without permission in writing from the publisher, except by a reviewer who may quote brief passages in a review.

First Edition: June 2023

Illustrations copyright © 2023 by Tanisha Owens Barrett

ISBN 979-8-218-24081-3 (hardcover)

Tanisha Owens Barrett
REALTOR®
eXp Realty
(864) 381-5324
www.tanishaowens.exprealty.com

"To all the home sellers who aspire to achieve a swift and successful sale, this book is dedicated to you and your journey towards unlocking the true potential of your homes.

To my dad, thank you for aspiring me to make a difference in the lives of those around me, just like you did."

Table of Contents

Prologue

Chapter 1: Why Selling Your Home Fast Matters

Chapter 2: Understanding the Real Estate Market

Chapter 3: Preparing Your Home for Sale

Chapter 4: Pricing Strategies for a Quick Sale

Chapter 5: Effective Marketing Techniques

Chapter 6: Maximizing Exposure

Chapter 7: Negotiating Offers and Closing the Deal

Chapter 8: Overcoming Common Challenges

Chapter 9: Working with Professionals

Chapter 10: Post-Sale Considerations

Chapter 11: Conclusion

About the Author

PROLOGUE

Whether you're a first-time home seller or someone experienced in the real estate market, this book is designed to equip you with the knowledge and strategies needed to sell your home swiftly, regardless of market conditions.

Selling a home can be a complex and overwhelming process, but with the right tools and techniques, it doesn't have to be. In these pages, you will find a comprehensive guide that will empower you to take control of your home sale and optimise your chances of achieving a fast and successful transaction.

As I'm sure you're aware: The real estate market is constantly evolving. It is influenced by economic factors, buyer preferences, and local dynamics. This book takes into account the latest market trends and provides you with proven strategies that work in any market, whether it's a seller's market, a buyer's market, or one that's just somewhere in-between.

Preparing your home for sale is a crucial first step, and we will delve into the importance of creating an appealing and inviting space that captures buyers' attention from the moment they step through the door. You'll learn how to stage your home effectively, make impactful repairs and renovations, and enhance your curb appeal to leave a lasting impression.

Pricing your home appropriately is another vital aspect of a fast sale. This book will guide you through the process of setting a competitive asking price, taking into account local comps, market trends, and the unique features of your property. You will also discover effective pricing strategies that will attract potential buyers and motivate them to make an offer FAST!

Marketing is also key in reaching a wide audience of potential buyers. In this book, we'll explore various marketing techniques and channels, from traditional methods to leveraging the power of online platforms and social media. You'll gain insights into crafting compelling listing descriptions, utilising professional photography, and implementing targeted marketing campaigns to maximise your home's exposure.

But selling your home quickly doesn't just stop at marketing. Negotiations play a critical role in securing a fast and favourable deal. This book will equip you with effective negotiation strategies, helping you navigate offers, counteroffers, and contingencies with confidence. Learn how to communicate effectively, maintain a win-win mindset, and close the deal smoothly.

Throughout this book, we'll also address common challenges you may encounter along the way and provide practical solutions to overcome them. From dealing with lowball offers to managing buyer objections, we'll guide you through potential hurdles, ensuring you're well-prepared to handle any situation that arises.

Additionally, we'll emphasise the importance of working with professionals, like myself, who can support you throughout the selling process. Whether it's choosing the right real estate agent, collaborating with home staging professionals, or partnering with mortgage brokers and attorneys, their expertise will prove invaluable in achieving a fast and successful sale.

As you embark on your home-selling journey, remember that selling a home quickly requires diligence, perseverance, and a proactive approach. This book will be your trusted companion, offering step-by-step guidance, practical tips, and expert insights to help you navigate the complexities of the real estate market and achieve your goal of selling your home fast.

So, without further a-due, let's dive in and empower you to become a confident and knowledgeable home seller, equipped with the tools and strategies to sell your home like a hot potato!

CHAPTER 1
WHY SELLING YOUR HOME FAST MATTERS

Selling a home quickly holds several significant advantages for homeowners. Here are some reasons why the speed of the home sale is important:

1. **Financial Benefits:** Selling your home quickly can help you avoid ongoing expenses associated with homeownership. These costs may include mortgage payments, property taxes, insurance, and maintenance expenses. By selling promptly, you can free up your financial resources and allocate them towards other investments or goals.

2. **Minimise Stress and Uncertainty:** The longer a home stays on the market, the more stress and uncertainty it can create for the homeowner. Extended selling periods can lead to increased anxiety, as homeowners worry about finding a buyer, maintaining the property for showings, and negotiating offers. Selling quickly can alleviate these concerns, allowing you to move forward

with your plans and transition to the next phase of your life.

3. **Capitalize on Market Conditions:** Real estate markets can be volatile, and conditions can change rapidly. Selling your home swiftly allows you to take advantage of favorable market conditions, such as high demand or low inventory. By capitalizing on these conditions, you may increase the likelihood of receiving competitive offers and maximizing your sale price.

4. **Enhanced Negotiating Power:** When a home is freshly listed, it tends to attract more attention from potential buyers. This increased interest can lead to a greater sense of urgency among buyers, potentially resulting in multiple offers or bidding wars. As a seller, having multiple interested parties can strengthen your negotiating position and increase the chances of securing a favorable deal.

5. **Reduced Holding Costs:** Holding onto a property for an extended period can result in additional expenses and potential financial risks. These costs can include mortgage interest, property taxes, maintenance, utilities, and insurance. By selling quickly, you can minimize or eliminate these ongoing holding costs, saving you money in the long run.

6. **Flexibility and Freedom:** Selling your home quickly grants you more flexibility and freedom to pursue new opportunities. Whether you're relocating for a job, downsizing, upsizing, or seeking a change of scenery, a fast home sale allows you to move forward with your

plans without being tied down by the burdens of an unsold property.

7. **Avoiding Stale Listings:** If a home remains on the market for an extended period, it can become stigmatized as a "stale listing." Buyers may perceive a property that has been listed for a long time as undesirable or flawed, leading to lower offers or a lack of interest. Selling quickly helps avoid this stigma, positioning your home as a fresh and attractive option for potential buyers.

In summary, selling a home quickly offers financial benefits, reduces stress, takes advantage of market conditions, enhances negotiating power, minimizes holding costs, provides flexibility, and helps avoid the negative effects of a stale listing. These factors collectively make the speed of the home sale an essential consideration for homeowners looking to maximize their selling experience and achieve their goals efficiently.

CHAPTER 2
UNDERSTANDING THE REAL ESTATE MARKET

FACTORS THAT INFLUENCE HOME SALES

Several factors influence home sales, and understanding these factors can help sellers make informed decisions and navigate the real estate market effectively. Here are some key factors that can influence the sale of a home:

1. **Location:** Location is one of the most significant factors affecting home sales. Factors such as proximity to amenities (schools, shopping centers, parks), transportation options, safety, and desirability of the neighborhood can all impact the attractiveness and value of a property.

2. **Market Conditions:** The overall state of the real estate market, whether it's a seller's market or a buyer's market, can greatly influence home sales. In a seller's

market, where demand exceeds supply, homes may sell quickly and at higher prices. In a buyer's market, where there is more inventory than demand, homes may take longer to sell, and prices may be more competitive.

3. **Economic Factors:** Economic conditions, such as interest rates, job growth, and overall economic stability, can influence home sales. Lower interest rates generally make home buying more affordable, potentially increasing demand. Conversely, economic downturns or job losses can dampen demand and slow down the pace of home sales.

4. **Home Condition and Appeal:** The condition and appeal of a home play a significant role in attracting buyers. Well-maintained properties that are move-in ready and visually appealing tend to generate more interest. Factors such as curb appeal, interior aesthetics, layout, functionality, and the presence of desired features (such as updated kitchens or bathrooms) can impact buyer perception and ultimately influence the sale.

5. **Pricing:** The pricing of a home is a crucial factor in attracting buyers and facilitating a sale. Homes priced too high relative to the market can deter potential buyers, while underpricing may raise suspicions or lead to missed opportunities. Setting a competitive and realistic asking price based on market conditions and comparable sales is essential to generating interest and receiving offers.

6. **Marketing and Exposure:** Effective marketing and exposure strategies can significantly impact home sales. Properly marketing a home through professional photography, online listings, virtual tours, open houses, and targeted advertising can help reach a broader audience of potential buyers and increase the likelihood of a quick sale.

7. **Timing:** The timing of when a home is listed for sale can influence its marketability. Seasonal variations, local market dynamics, and current trends can all impact buyer interest. Understanding when the market is most active in your area and strategically timing your listing can increase the chances of a faster sale.

8. **Home Improvements and Staging:** Making necessary repairs, updates, or improvements to a home can enhance its appeal and market value. Additionally, professional home staging can help showcase the property's potential, allowing buyers to envision themselves living in the space. These factors can positively influence buyer perception and expedite the selling process.

9. **Real Estate Professionals:** The expertise and guidance of real estate professionals, such as agents, brokers, and appraisers, can influence home sales. Working with experienced professionals who have knowledge of the local market and a network of potential buyers can help sellers navigate the complexities of the sales process and increase the likelihood of a successful transaction.

It's important to note that the influence of these factors can vary based on local market conditions and individual circumstances. Consulting with a real estate professional can provide valuable insights specific to your situation and location.

SETTING REALISTIC EXPECTATIONS

Setting realistic expectations when selling your home is crucial for a smooth and successful selling experience. Here are some key steps to help you set realistic expectations:

1. **Research the Market:** Begin by researching the current real estate market in your area. Understand whether it's a seller's market, a buyer's market, or a balanced market. Analyze recent sales data, average time on the market, and pricing trends. This research will give you a better understanding of what to expect in terms of timing and pricing for your home sale.

2. **Consult with Real Estate Professionals:** Seek guidance from experienced real estate professionals,

such as agents or brokers, who have expertise in your local market. They can provide insights into current market conditions, comparable sales, and realistic pricing expectations. They will also help you understand the process, potential challenges, and timelines involved in selling your home.

3. **Assess Your Home's Condition:** Evaluate your home objectively to determine its condition and any potential issues that might impact its marketability. Consider getting a pre-listing inspection to identify and address any repairs or maintenance needs. Understanding the condition of your home will help you set realistic expectations about its value and potential buyer concerns.

4. **Consider Comparable Sales:** Examine recent sales of similar homes in your neighborhood, often referred to as "comps." Look at properties that are similar in size, age, features, and location. This analysis will provide insights into the pricing range and expectations for your home. Consider factors such as sold prices, days on the market, and any unique features or upgrades that may impact value.

5. **Evaluate Your Home's Unique Features and Upgrades:** Take stock of any unique features or upgrades your home offers compared to other properties on the market. These features can positively influence the perceived value of your home and potentially justify a higher price. However, it's essential to be realistic about the additional value these features

bring and how they align with buyer preferences in your market.

6. **Understand Buyer Preferences:** Familiarize yourself with the preferences of potential buyers in your area. Consider factors such as architectural styles, popular amenities, school districts, transportation access, and neighborhood characteristics. Being aware of buyer preferences will help you align your expectations with market demand.

7. **Analyze Timeframe Considerations:** Consider your personal timeline and any external factors that may impact the sale of your home. Are you in a rush to sell due to a job relocation or other life circumstances? Are there seasonal factors that may affect buyer interest in your area? Understanding these considerations will help you set realistic expectations for the timing of your home sale.

8. **Factor in Negotiations and Market Conditions:** Recognize that negotiations and market conditions can impact the final sale price of your home. Be prepared for potential back-and-forth negotiations with buyers and understand that the initial offer may not match your asking price. Take into account potential contingencies, such as appraisal outcomes or financing issues, which may affect the final sale price or the closing timeline.

9. **Be Open to Adjustments:** Realize that the real estate market can be unpredictable, and adjustments may be necessary along the way. If you find that your initial pricing or marketing strategy isn't generating sufficient

interest, be open to reassessing and making adjustments. This flexibility will help you adapt to market feedback and set more realistic expectations.

CHAPTER 3

PREPARING YOUR HOME FOR SALE

ASSESSING YOUR HOME'S CONDITION

Assessing your home's condition is an important step when preparing to sell. Here's a guide to help you assess your home's condition effectively:

1. **Exterior Evaluation:**

    1. Start by examining the exterior of your home. Look for any visible signs of damage or wear, such as cracks in the foundation, damaged siding, or loose roof shingles. Take note of any areas that need attention or repairs.

    2. Assess the condition of the landscaping, including the lawn, trees, and shrubs. Ensure that the yard is well-maintained, with trimmed bushes, weeded flower beds, and healthy vegetation. Curb appeal plays a significant role in attracting potential buyers.

3. Check the condition of the driveway, walkways, and exterior structures like decks or patios. Look for cracks, uneven surfaces, or any signs of deterioration that may need to be addressed.

2. **Interior Evaluation:**

    1. Begin with a room-by-room assessment. Examine the walls, ceilings, and floors for any signs of damage, such as cracks, water stains, or peeling paint. Check for any structural issues or signs of pests.

    2. Inspect the functionality and condition of doors, windows, and locks. Ensure they open and close smoothly and that all mechanisms are in working order.

    3. Evaluate the condition of the electrical system, including outlets, switches, and light fixtures. Ensure everything is in good working condition and up to code.

    4. Check the plumbing system for any leaks, drips, or issues with faucets, toilets, and drains. Look for water stains or signs of water damage.

    5. Evaluate the HVAC system (heating, ventilation, and air conditioning) to ensure it's functioning properly. Consider having it professionally serviced if needed.

6. Assess the condition of flooring, including carpets, hardwood, or tiles. Look for any stains, wear, or necessary repairs. Consider cleaning or refinishing surfaces to improve their appearance.

3. **Kitchen and Bathrooms:**

    1. Pay special attention to the kitchen and bathrooms, as these areas often have a significant impact on buyers' perceptions.

    2. Evaluate the condition of countertops, cabinets, and appliances. Check for any damage, scratches, or outdated features. Consider whether any updates or repairs are necessary to improve the overall appeal.

    3. Inspect plumbing fixtures, such as faucets, sinks, and toilets, for leaks or signs of wear. Ensure that all plumbing is functioning properly.

4. **Maintenance and Repairs:**

    1. Make a list of necessary repairs and maintenance tasks based on your assessments. This may include fixing leaky faucets, repairing damaged walls, replacing broken tiles, or addressing any structural issues.

    2. Consider scheduling a professional home inspection to get a comprehensive assessment of your home's

condition. A home inspector can identify any hidden issues or areas that need attention.

5. **Cosmetic Improvements:**

    1. Evaluate the overall aesthetics of your home's interior and exterior. Consider if any cosmetic improvements, such as fresh paint, updated fixtures, or improved lighting, would enhance its appeal to potential buyers.

HOME STAGING TECHNIQUES FOR MAXIMUM APPEAL

Home staging is a valuable technique for presenting your home in the best possible light to potential buyers. Here are some home staging techniques to maximize its appeal:

1. **Declutter and Depersonalize:**

    1. Start by decluttering your home. Remove unnecessary items, such as excessive furniture, personal belongings, and knick-knacks. Clearing out clutter

helps create a sense of space and allows buyers to envision themselves in the home.

2. Depersonalize by removing personal photographs, unique artwork, and personalized items. This helps buyers focus on the home itself rather than the current occupants.

2. Deep Clean:

A clean and fresh home creates a positive impression. Thoroughly clean every room, including windows, floors, carpets, countertops, and bathrooms. Pay attention to details, such as grout lines, fixtures, and appliances.

3. Neutralize Paint Colors:

Neutral paint colors create a blank canvas for potential buyers and help them visualize their own style and preferences. Consider repainting any bold or personalized colors with neutral tones that have broad appeal.

4. Maximize Natural Light:

Open curtains and blinds to maximize natural light. Well-lit spaces feel more welcoming and spacious. Clean windows to allow as much light as possible to enter the rooms.

5. **Furniture Arrangement and Space Planning:**

    1. Arrange furniture in a way that creates a sense of flow and highlights the functionality of each room. Avoid blocking natural pathways and ensure that furniture is appropriately scaled for the space.

    2. Consider removing or rearranging furniture to create a more open and spacious feel. Less furniture can make rooms appear larger.

6. **Highlight Key Features:**

    Showcase the unique selling points of your home. If you have a beautiful fireplace, architectural details, or scenic views, make sure they are highlighted and unobstructed. Use furniture placement, artwork, or accessories to draw attention to these features.

7. **Create Inviting Ambiance:**

    1. Use soft lighting, such as table lamps or floor lamps, to create a warm and inviting ambiance. Lighting can enhance the atmosphere and make spaces feel cozy and comfortable.

    2. Consider adding pleasant scents, such as freshly baked cookies or subtle candles, to create a welcoming aroma.

8. **Enhance Curb Appeal:**

    First impressions matter, so pay attention to your home's exterior. Ensure the front yard is well-maintained, the landscaping is tidy, and the entryway is clean and inviting. Consider adding potted plants or fresh flowers near the entrance to add a touch of color and freshness.

9. **Style Each Room:**

1. Style each room purposefully to showcase its potential. Use tasteful accessories, such as decorative pillows, artwork, or rugs, to add visual interest and make each space feel inviting.

2. Use cohesive color schemes and textures to create a harmonious and unified look throughout the home.

10. **Outdoor Living Spaces:**

If you have outdoor living spaces, stage them as an extension of the home. Set up outdoor furniture, arrange cozy seating areas, and add decorative elements like cushions or potted plants. This helps buyers envision the potential for outdoor entertaining or relaxation.

REPAIRS AND RENOVATIONS THAT YIELD HIGH RETURNS

When considering repairs and renovations to maximize the return on your investment, it's important to focus on projects that appeal to a broad range of buyers and provide a significant value boost to your home. While the return on investment can vary depending on factors such as location, market conditions, and the specific property, here are some repairs and renovations that tend to yield a higher return:

1. **Kitchen Remodeling:** The kitchen is often considered the heart of the home, and updates in this area can have a significant impact. Focus on improvements that enhance functionality and aesthetics, such as replacing outdated appliances, upgrading countertops, cabinets, and backsplash, and adding modern fixtures. A well-executed kitchen remodel can yield a high return on investment.

2. **Bathroom Upgrades:** Updating bathrooms is another renovation project that often provides a good return. Consider replacing worn-out fixtures, upgrading lighting, installing new tiles or flooring, and improving storage options. Adding modern touches and creating a

spa-like atmosphere can greatly appeal to potential buyers.

3. **Curb Appeal Enhancements:** First impressions matter, and enhancing your home's curb appeal can yield a high return. Consider projects such as repainting the exterior, upgrading the front door, improving landscaping, and installing outdoor lighting. These improvements can make your home more visually appealing and inviting.

4. **Energy-Efficient Improvements:** Increasing energy efficiency not only benefits the environment but can also be attractive to buyers. Upgrades like installing energy-efficient windows, improving insulation, upgrading HVAC systems, and adding smart thermostats or solar panels can lower utility bills and make your home more appealing to eco-conscious buyers.

5. **Flooring Upgrades:** Replacing worn-out or outdated flooring can have a significant impact on the perceived value of your home. Consider installing hardwood flooring, which is highly desirable to buyers. Alternatively, high-quality laminate or tile flooring can provide a cost-effective solution while still improving the overall look and feel of your home.

6. **Basement Renovation:** If you have an unfinished basement, renovating it can significantly increase your home's living space and appeal. Transforming it into a functional living area, such as a recreation room, home office, or additional bedroom, can add value and attract

potential buyers looking for more usable square footage.

7. **Minor Cosmetic Enhancements:** Simple and cost-effective cosmetic enhancements can go a long way in making your home more appealing. Consider repainting the interior walls with neutral colors, replacing outdated light fixtures, updating door handles and hardware, and refreshing the overall look with new window treatments.

8. **Maintenance and Repairs:** Addressing necessary maintenance and repairs is essential. Fixing leaky faucets, repairing damaged walls, replacing broken tiles, and addressing any structural issues helps ensure that your home is in good condition and minimizes potential buyer concerns.

∎∎

Your return on investment can vary depending on your specific market and the quality of the renovations. It's essential to carefully consider your budget, consult with real estate professionals, and focus on improvements that align with the preferences of potential buyers in your area.

ENHANCING CURB APPEAL

Enhancing the curb appeal of your home is an effective way to make a positive first impression and attract potential buyers. Here are some tips to enhance the curb appeal of your home:

1. **Maintain a Well-Manicured Lawn:** Regularly mow the lawn, trim the edges, and remove any weeds. Keep the grass healthy by watering and fertilizing appropriately. Patch any bare spots and consider adding fresh sod if needed.

2. **Add Vibrant Landscaping:** Plant colorful flowers, shrubs, and plants to add visual interest and a pop of color. Choose varieties that thrive in your climate and complement the style of your home. Consider using planters or hanging baskets to add height and dimension.

3. **Define and Tidy Garden Beds:** Edge garden beds to create clean lines and separate them from the lawn. Remove any weeds, dead plants, or debris. Apply fresh mulch or bark to give the beds a polished and well-maintained appearance.

4. **Trim Trees and Shrubs:** Prune overgrown trees and shrubs to create a neat and tidy look. Ensure that they don't obstruct windows, walkways, or the view of the

house. Removing dead branches or overgrowth can improve the overall appearance of your property.

5. **Enhance the Front Entrance:** The front entrance is a focal point, so make it inviting and visually appealing. Consider painting the front door in a bold color that complements the exterior. Add a new doormat, a potted plant, or hanging baskets on the porch for a welcoming touch.

6. **Upgrade Lighting:** Install attractive outdoor lighting fixtures to illuminate the pathways, entryway, and key features of your home. Well-placed lighting enhances safety and creates an inviting ambiance, especially during evening showings.

7. **Clean Exterior Surfaces:** Power wash the exterior walls, driveway, and sidewalks to remove dirt, grime, and stains. Clean the windows inside and out to make them sparkle. This helps create a fresh and well-maintained appearance.

8. **Repaint or Touch Up:** Consider repainting the exterior of your home if the current paint is faded or peeling. Choose neutral or classic colors that appeal to a broad range of buyers. If repainting the entire house is not feasible, touch up areas with noticeable wear or discoloration.

9. **Upgrade House Numbers and Mailbox:** Replace worn-out or outdated house numbers and the mailbox to freshen up the look. Choose stylish and easily

readable designs that complement the architectural style of your home.

10. **Hide Unsightly Elements:** Conceal or camouflage unsightly elements such as air conditioning units, propane tanks, or garbage bins. Use strategic landscaping, fencing, or decorative screens to create a more visually appealing view.

11. **Repair and Paint Fences or Gates:** Ensure that fences or gates are in good condition. Repair any damages and give them a fresh coat of paint or stain if necessary. Well-maintained fencing adds charm and enhances the overall curb appeal.

12. **Pay Attention to Details:** Small details can make a big difference. Consider upgrading or cleaning the front porch light fixtures, doorbell, house nameplate, or any other decorative elements. These minor improvements can give your home a polished look.

■■

Enhancing the curb appeal is about creating a welcoming and well-maintained exterior that entices potential buyers to explore further. Regular maintenance and attention to detail can go a long way in making your home stand out in a positive way.

CHAPTER 4
PRICING STRATEGIES FOR A QUICK SALE

IMPORTANCE OF PRICING RIGHT

Pricing your home right is crucial because it directly impacts your ability to sell your home quickly and for the best possible price. Here are the key reasons why pricing your home correctly is important:

1. **Attracting Potential Buyers:** Setting the right price for your home increases the chances of attracting a larger pool of potential buyers. When a home is priced competitively, it stands out in the market and generates more interest. This can lead to more inquiries, showings, and ultimately, offers on your property.

2. **Minimizing Time on the Market:** Overpricing your home can result in it sitting on the market for an extended period. The longer a home remains unsold, the more likely buyers and real estate professionals will

question its value or assume there are underlying issues. Pricing your home appropriately increases the likelihood of a faster sale, reducing the time and stress associated with a prolonged selling process.

3. **Maximizing Buyer Interest:** A well-priced home tends to generate more interest among potential buyers. When buyers perceive a property to be reasonably priced, they are more motivated to schedule showings and make offers. Increased buyer interest can lead to multiple offers and potentially drive up the final sale price.

4. **Setting Realistic Expectations:** Proper pricing helps manage the expectations of both sellers and buyers. Overpricing can create unrealistic expectations for sellers, resulting in disappointment and missed opportunities. On the other hand, pricing your home accurately helps set realistic expectations for buyers regarding the value they can expect from the property.

5. **Attracting Serious Buyers:** Pricing your home correctly helps attract serious buyers who are actively looking in your price range. Serious buyers are more likely to conduct thorough research, visit the property, and make competitive offers. By pricing your home competitively, you increase the chances of engaging with motivated and qualified buyers.

6. **Avoiding Appraisal Issues:** An appraisal is typically required when a buyer is obtaining financing for the purchase. If your home is overpriced, it may not appraise for the desired value. This can lead to

complications in the financing process and potentially result in the deal falling through. Pricing your home accurately helps ensure a smoother transaction and avoids appraisal-related issues.

7. **Maximizing Negotiation Power:** Pricing your home right can give you more negotiation power during the selling process. When a home is priced appropriately, buyers are more likely to perceive it as a fair deal. This can lead to more productive negotiations, where both parties feel they are getting a fair value for the property.

■■

It's important to work with a knowledgeable real estate agent or conduct thorough market research to determine the right price for your home. A professional can provide you with a comparative market analysis (CMA) and valuable insights into local market conditions, helping you set the optimal price to maximize your chances of a successful sale.

DETERMINING A COMPETITIVE ASKING PRICE

Determining a competitive asking price for your home requires careful consideration of various factors. Here are steps to help you determine an appropriate asking price:

1. **Research Comparable Sales:** Begin by researching recent sales of similar homes in your area. Look for properties with similar features, such as size, location, number of bedrooms/bathrooms, and amenities. Pay attention to sale prices, as well as the time it took for these homes to sell. This information will give you a benchmark for pricing your own home.

2. **Conduct a Comparative Market Analysis (CMA):** A CMA is a more detailed analysis conducted by a real estate agent. They will evaluate comparable sales, active listings, and expired listings to provide a comprehensive picture of the market. A CMA takes into account factors such as market trends, demand, and the unique characteristics of your property. Consider consulting with a local real estate agent to assist you in preparing a CMA.

3. **Evaluate Current Market Conditions:** Assess the current state of the real estate market in your area. Is it a buyer's market, a seller's market, or balanced? In a seller's market with limited inventory and high demand, you may have more flexibility in pricing. In a buyer's

market with more supply and less demand, pricing competitively becomes even more crucial.

4. **Consider Unique Features and Upgrades:** Take into account any unique features or upgrades your home offers that differentiate it from the competition. These can include renovated kitchens, updated bathrooms, energy-efficient upgrades, or desirable outdoor spaces. These features may justify a slightly higher asking price.

5. **Factor in the Condition of Your Home:** Be honest about the condition of your home. Consider any necessary repairs or updates that may affect its value. A well-maintained and move-in ready home typically commands a higher price than one requiring significant repairs.

6. **Get a Professional Appraisal:** If you want an objective assessment of your home's value, consider hiring a professional appraiser. Appraisers evaluate various factors, including the property's condition, location, size, and recent sales data to determine an unbiased value.

7. **Be Mindful of Overpricing:** While it may be tempting to set a higher price in hopes of negotiating down, overpricing your home can deter potential buyers and lead to extended time on the market. Buyers and their agents often have a good understanding of the local market and may disregard overpriced listings.

8. **Seek Advice from a Real Estate Professional:** Real estate agents have in-depth knowledge of local market

conditions and pricing strategies. They can provide guidance based on their expertise and experience. Consult with a reputable agent who has a track record of success in your area to help you determine a competitive asking price.

∎∎

Setting the right asking price is a delicate balance. Pricing too high can discourage buyers, while pricing too low may result in leaving money on the table. Utilize available resources, consult professionals, and carefully analyze market data to arrive at a competitive asking price that reflects the true value of your home.

PRICING STRATEGIES FOR DIFFERENT MARKET CONDITIONS

Pricing strategies can vary depending on the market conditions you are facing. Here are some common pricing strategies for different market scenarios:

1. **Seller's Market:**

   1. **Set a Slightly Higher Price:** In a seller's market with limited inventory and high demand, you may have the flexibility to set a slightly higher asking price. Buyers may be willing to pay a premium for desirable properties.

   2. **Consider a "Coming Soon" Strategy:** Generating anticipation by listing your property as "Coming Soon" before it officially hits the market can create a sense of exclusivity and attract motivated buyers who are eager to make an offer.

   3. **Review and Respond to Multiple Offers:** In a seller's market, it's common to receive multiple offers. Evaluate each offer carefully, considering not only the price but also the terms and conditions. Engage in negotiations to maximize your return.

2. **Buyer's Market:**

    1. **Price Competitively:** In a buyer's market with more supply and less demand, pricing competitively becomes crucial. Setting a reasonable and attractive price can help generate interest and stand out among other listings.

    2. **Offer Incentives:** Consider offering incentives such as seller concessions, covering closing costs, or including certain appliances or furniture in the sale. These incentives can make your property more appealing to potential buyers.

    3. **Be Flexible on Negotiations:** In a market favoring buyers, be open to negotiating on price and terms. Consider offers that are slightly below your asking price and be willing to find common ground during negotiations.

3. **Balanced Market:**

    1. **Analyze Comparable Sales:** In a balanced market, where supply and demand are relatively equal, analyze recent comparable sales to determine a fair and competitive asking price. Pay attention to factors such as location, size, condition, and unique features of your property.

    2. **Highlight Unique Selling Points:** Emphasize the unique selling points of your property to differentiate it from others on the market. Showcase any recent upgrades, desirable amenities, or sought-after

neighborhood features that make your home stand out.

3. **Monitor Market Trends:** Stay updated on market trends and adjust your pricing strategy accordingly. If you notice shifts in buyer preferences or changes in supply and demand dynamics, be prepared to adapt your pricing approach.

4. **Luxury Market:**

    1. **Price for Prestige and Exclusivity:** In the luxury market, pricing is often based on the prestige and exclusivity of the property. Highlight the high-end features, luxurious finishes, and premium amenities to justify the price.

    2. **Market to a Targeted Audience:** Luxury properties often require a targeted marketing approach. Collaborate with real estate agents who specialize in the luxury market and utilize channels such as luxury publications, online platforms, and exclusive networks to reach potential buyers.

    3. **Be Patient and Flexible:** Selling luxury properties can take longer due to the smaller pool of qualified buyers. Be patient and prepared to adjust your pricing and marketing strategy as needed.

∎∎

Again, consult with a knowledgeable real estate professional who can provide specific insights and guidance based on the current market conditions in your area. They can help you navigate the pricing strategies that align with your goals and the dynamics of the market you are operating in.

THE IMPACT OF LOCAL COMPS AND APPRAISALS

Local comps (comparable sales) and appraisals have a significant impact on the sale of a home. Here's an overview of their importance:

1. **Local Comps:**

    1. **Pricing Guidance:** Local comps provide valuable data on recent sales of similar properties in your area. They serve as a benchmark for determining the fair market value of your home. By analyzing the sale prices of comparable properties, you can get a better understanding of what buyers are willing to pay.

    2. **Market Awareness:** Local comps help you gain insights into the current market conditions and trends. Understanding how homes similar to yours are performing in terms of pricing, days on market, and buyer demand can inform your pricing strategy.

    3. **Appraiser Considerations:** When an appraiser evaluates your home, they will consider local comps as part of their assessment. These comparables help the appraiser determine the value of your property based on recent sales in the area.

2. **Appraisals:**

    1. **Objective Property Valuation:** Appraisals provide an objective assessment of a property's value by a licensed appraiser. Lenders typically require an appraisal to determine whether the property's value supports the loan amount. The appraiser considers various factors such as the property's condition, size, location, and comparable sales to arrive at a fair market value.

    2. **Mortgage Financing:** Appraisals play a crucial role in mortgage financing. Lenders rely on appraisals to ensure they are not lending more than the property is worth. If the appraisal comes in lower than the agreed-upon purchase price, it can lead to challenges with financing and potentially require renegotiation between the buyer and seller.

    3. **Sale Price Validation:** Appraisals provide an independent validation of the sale price. They help ensure that the buyer is not overpaying for the property and that the seller is receiving a fair value. Appraisals can help facilitate a smooth transaction by establishing confidence in the property's value for both parties involved.

∎∎

Both local comps and appraisals contribute to establishing a realistic and fair market value for your home. They provide valuable information to guide your pricing decisions, support negotiations, and satisfy lender requirements. It's important to work with a knowledgeable real estate professional who can assist you in evaluating local comps and preparing for the appraisal process to ensure you price your home accurately and navigate the selling process successfully.

CHAPTER 5
EFFECTIVE MARKETING TECHNIQUES

CRAFTING AN ATTRACTIVE LISTING DESCRIPTION

Crafting an attractive listing description is essential to capture the attention of potential buyers and generate interest in your home. Here are some tips to help you create an appealing listing description:

1. **Highlight Key Features:** Start by showcasing the most desirable features of your home. Whether it's a spacious backyard, a newly renovated kitchen, or a stunning view, highlight these unique selling points early in the description to grab the reader's attention.

2. **Use Engaging Language:** Write in a way that captivates readers and sparks their imagination. Use descriptive and vivid language to paint a picture of the lifestyle your home offers. Instead of simply stating

facts, evoke emotions and create a sense of excitement about the property.

3. **Be Specific and Detailed:** Provide specific details about the property, including the number of bedrooms and bathrooms, square footage, lot size, and any notable amenities. Potential buyers want to know the specifics to determine if the home meets their needs and preferences.

4. **Emphasize Upgrades and Renovations:** If you've made any recent upgrades or renovations, highlight them in the listing description. Mention new appliances, flooring, fixtures, or any other features that add value to the property.

5. **Tell a Story:** Craft a narrative that connects with potential buyers. Describe how the home has been a haven for family gatherings, a place for making cherished memories, or a peaceful retreat. Engage the reader by making them envision themselves living in the space.

6. **Use Proper Formatting and Structure:** Ensure that your listing description is easy to read and visually appealing. Use bullet points to highlight key features, and break up paragraphs into shorter, digestible sections. Use bold or italic fonts to draw attention to important details.

7. **Include Neighborhood and Location Information:** Describe the neighborhood and nearby amenities, such as parks, schools, shopping centers, or popular

attractions. Highlight the convenience and desirability of the location to attract buyers looking for a specific lifestyle or location.

8. **Utilize High-Quality Photos:** Pair your listing description with high-quality, professional photos that showcase the best features of your home. Visuals can greatly enhance the appeal of your listing and provide potential buyers with a clearer understanding of the property.

9. **Proofread and Edit:** Ensure your listing description is free from grammatical errors and typos. Proofread the content multiple times and consider having someone else review it as well. A well-written and error-free description demonstrates professionalism and attention to detail.

10. **Be Honest and Accurate:** While it's important to highlight the positive aspects of your home, be honest and accurate in your description. Avoid exaggerations or misleading statements, as it can lead to disappointment and frustration for potential buyers.

■■

Remember, your listing description serves as a powerful marketing tool to attract buyers. Take the time to craft a compelling and engaging narrative that accurately represents your home's unique features and lifestyle appeal.

UTILIZING PROFESSIONAL PHOTOGRAPHY AND VIRTUAL TOURS

Utilizing professional photography and virtual tours can greatly enhance the marketing of your home and attract potential buyers. Here's how you can make the most of these visual tools:

1. **Hire a Professional Photographer:** Invest in a professional photographer who specializes in real estate photography. Their expertise in capturing the best angles, lighting, and composition will result in high-quality images that showcase your home in its best possible light. Professional photos can significantly impact the first impression buyers have of your property.

2. **Stage Your Home:** Before the photography session, ensure your home is properly staged and decluttered. Clear away personal items and unnecessary clutter to create a clean and appealing environment. Consider adding tasteful decor and furniture arrangements that highlight the space's potential. Staging helps create visually appealing images that resonate with potential buyers.

3. **Capture Key Features:** Communicate with your photographer about the important features you want to highlight. Whether it's a spacious living room, a modern

kitchen, or a stunning backyard, make sure these areas are captured effectively. Showcase unique architectural details, upgraded finishes, and any other selling points that set your home apart.

4. **Use Natural Light:** Natural light can enhance the warmth and appeal of your home in photographs. Schedule the photography session during daylight hours when the natural light is abundant. Open curtains and blinds to let in as much light as possible. Avoid using flash photography, as it can create harsh lighting and unnatural shadows.

5. **Consider Aerial Photography:** If your property features unique outdoor spaces, large grounds, or attractive surroundings, aerial photography can provide a captivating perspective. Hiring a professional drone photographer can showcase your property's exterior, landscape, and nearby amenities from an elevated vantage point.

6. **Virtual Tours:** Virtual tours are an effective way to offer an immersive experience to potential buyers. Consider creating a virtual tour that allows viewers to explore your home online. Virtual tours can be interactive, allowing viewers to navigate through different rooms and get a sense of the flow and layout of the property. Hire a professional virtual tour provider or use dedicated virtual tour software to create an engaging and user-friendly experience.

7. **360-Degree Photos:** Incorporate 360-degree photos alongside traditional static images. These photos enable

viewers to explore the space from various angles, providing a more interactive and realistic feel. They offer a dynamic way to showcase the layout and features of your home.

8. **Promote on Online Platforms:** Once you have professional photos and virtual tours ready, use them strategically in your online marketing efforts. Include them in your listing on real estate websites, social media platforms, and other online marketing channels. These visuals will attract attention and entice potential buyers to learn more about your property.

Professional photography and virtual tours are powerful tools that can significantly enhance the presentation of your home. Utilize them effectively to create a visually appealing and immersive experience for potential buyers, ultimately increasing the chances of generating interest and securing showings.

LEVERAGING ONLINE PLATFORMS AND SOCIAL MEDIA

Leveraging online platforms and social media is crucial for reaching a wider audience and maximizing exposure when selling your home. Here are some strategies to effectively utilize these platforms:

1. **Choose the Right Online Platforms:** Start by selecting the most relevant and widely used online platforms for real estate listings. Popular options include real estate websites like Zillow, Realtor.com, and Trulia. Additionally, consider utilizing local real estate websites or listing services that cater to your specific region.

2. **Create a Compelling Listing:** Craft a compelling and detailed listing description that highlights the unique features and selling points of your home. Include high-quality professional photos and, if possible, a virtual tour. Make sure to provide accurate information about the property's specifications, location, amenities, and any recent renovations or upgrades.

3. **Share on Social Media:** Utilize your social media networks to reach a broader audience. Share your listing on platforms such as Facebook, Instagram, Twitter, and LinkedIn. Craft engaging posts with eye-catching visuals and a brief description of the property.

Encourage your friends, family, and connections to share your post to expand its reach.

4. **Utilize Real Estate Groups and Communities:** Join relevant real estate groups and communities on social media platforms. These groups often have members who are actively searching for homes or who may know someone in the market. Engage with these communities by sharing your listing and participating in discussions related to real estate.

5. **Use Hashtags:** Incorporate popular and relevant hashtags in your social media posts to increase visibility. Utilize hashtags such as #realestate, #homesforsale, #justlisted, and location-specific hashtags to target potential buyers who are actively searching for properties in your area.

6. **Engage with Local Influencers and Real Estate Agents:** Connect with local influencers or real estate agents who have a significant presence on social media. Collaborate with them to promote your listing or ask for a feature on their platforms. Their reach and influence can help expose your property to a larger audience.

7. **Consider Paid Advertising:** Explore paid advertising options on social media platforms. Platforms like Facebook and Instagram offer targeted advertising tools that allow you to reach specific demographics, interests, and geographical locations. Set a budget and create appealing ad campaigns that drive traffic to your listing or website.

8. **Monitor and Respond to Inquiries:** Stay actively engaged with online platforms by regularly monitoring and responding to inquiries and comments promptly. Answer questions, provide additional information, and schedule showings as necessary. Being responsive and professional helps build trust and encourages potential buyers to take the next steps.

■■

Always prioritize safety when utilizing online platforms. Be cautious about sharing personal information and consider meeting potential buyers in a public place or having your real estate agent present during showings. By effectively leveraging online platforms and social media, you can significantly increase the visibility of your home, attract a larger pool of potential buyers, and ultimately increase the chances of a successful sale.

TARGETED MARKETING TO REACH POTENTIAL BUYERS

Targeted marketing is essential for reaching potential buyers and increasing the chances of a successful sale. Here are some strategies to target your marketing efforts effectively:

1. **Identify Your Target Audience:** Start by understanding who your ideal buyers are. Consider factors such as demographics, lifestyle preferences, and the type of property you are selling. Are you targeting young professionals, families, retirees, or investors? Understanding your target audience helps tailor your marketing messages and select the right marketing channels.

2. **Highlight Key Selling Points:** Determine the unique selling points of your property that would appeal to your target audience. Are you located in a family-friendly neighborhood with excellent schools nearby? Does your property offer modern amenities or a tranquil retreat? Highlight these features in your marketing materials to attract the right buyers.

3. **Utilize Online Marketing:** Leverage online marketing channels to target potential buyers effectively. Use real estate websites, social media platforms, and search engine advertising to reach a broader audience. Utilize

targeting options available on these platforms to refine your audience based on location, demographics, interests, and behaviors.

4. **Local Marketing:** Focus on local marketing efforts to attract buyers who are specifically interested in your area. Advertise in local newspapers, community magazines, and real estate publications. Collaborate with local businesses, such as coffee shops or restaurants, to display flyers or brochures about your property. Target local networking events and community gatherings to spread the word about your home.

5. **Professional Networks:** Leverage the professional networks of your real estate agent. Experienced agents have access to a network of potential buyers and other real estate professionals. They can market your property to their network, which may include individuals actively searching for properties or those who work closely with buyers.

6. **Open Houses and Private Showings:** Organize open houses and private showings to attract potential buyers. Advertise these events through targeted online platforms, local publications, and real estate websites. Consider hosting themed open houses, such as a Sunday brunch or an evening cocktail party, to create a memorable experience for visitors.

7. **Collaborate with Real Estate Agents:** Partner with real estate agents who specialize in selling properties similar to yours. They have access to a database of potential buyers and can market your property directly to their

client base. Their expertise in understanding buyer preferences and effective marketing strategies can greatly enhance your reach.

8. **Direct Mail and Print Advertising:** Consider targeted direct mail campaigns to reach potential buyers. Create visually appealing brochures or postcards that highlight the best features of your property. Use targeted mailing lists based on location, demographics, or specific interests. Additionally, place advertisements in local newspapers, real estate magazines, or neighborhood newsletters to increase visibility.

9. **Online Listing Enhancements:** Make use of enhanced features and upgrades available on real estate websites. These features often include options for premium placement, featured listings, or additional photos and descriptions. Investing in these upgrades can increase the visibility of your listing and attract more potential buyers.

■■

Don't forget to track the performance of your marketing efforts to identify which channels and strategies are generating the most interest. Continually refine your marketing approach based on the results and feedback you receive. By targeting your marketing efforts towards the right audience, you increase the likelihood of connecting with motivated buyers who are genuinely interested in your property.

CHAPTER 6

MAXIMIZING EXPOSURE

OPEN HOUSES AND PRIVATE SHOWINGS

To maximize home exposure through open houses and private showings, follow these tips:

1. **Prepare the Home:** Prior to any showings, ensure your home is clean, decluttered, and well-maintained. Make necessary repairs, touch up paint, and address any cosmetic issues. Stage the home to highlight its best features and create a welcoming atmosphere.

2. **Professional Photography:** Capture high-quality professional photographs of your home's interior and exterior to use in promotional materials and online listings. These visuals will attract potential buyers and generate interest before they even visit the property.

3. **Create Inviting Signage:** Place attractive signage in front of your property to catch the attention of passersby. Use clear and professional signage that includes essential information such as the date and time

of the open house or a contact number for private showings.

4. **Advertise Effectively:** Utilize various marketing channels to advertise your open house and private showings. Leverage online platforms, social media, real estate websites, and local publications to reach a wide audience. Craft compelling listing descriptions and include attractive photos to entice potential buyers to attend.

5. **Timing and Scheduling:** Choose the most convenient time and day for open houses and private showings. Consider weekends or evenings when more buyers may be available to visit. Provide flexibility for private showings to accommodate potential buyers' schedules.

6. **Provide Informational Materials:** Prepare informational materials such as brochures or property fact sheets to provide visitors with details about your home. Include key features, recent upgrades, floor plans, and any relevant neighborhood information. Ensure that contact information is easily accessible for potential buyers to reach out with inquiries.

7. **Stage for Success:** Stage your home strategically to create an appealing ambiance during open houses and private showings. Set up furniture and decor to showcase each room's purpose and potential. Consider adding fresh flowers, subtle scents, or soft background music to create a welcoming atmosphere.

8. **Engage with Visitors:** Greet and engage with visitors during open houses and private showings. Be knowledgeable about your property and prepared to answer questions. Provide insight into the neighborhood, nearby amenities, and any potential future development plans that could increase the property's value.

9. **Offer Refreshments:** Consider providing light refreshments such as water, coffee, or snacks during open houses. This small gesture can make visitors feel more comfortable and encourage them to spend more time exploring your home.

10. **Follow-Up:** Follow up with potential buyers who attended the open house or private showings. Send a personalized email thanking them for their visit and offer to provide additional information or schedule a follow-up showing if they express interest.

11. **Request Feedback:** Ask for feedback from visitors regarding their impressions of the home. This feedback can help you identify areas for improvement or address any concerns that may arise during the showing process.

■■

By implementing these strategies, you can maximize home exposure during open houses and private showings, increase interest from potential buyers, and ultimately improve the chances of a successful sale.

USING SIGNAGE AND FLYERS EFFECTIVELY

Signage and flyers are effective marketing tools that can help generate interest and attract potential buyers when selling your home. Here's how to use them effectively:

1. **Eye-Catching Signage:** Place a visible and attractive "For Sale" sign in your front yard. Make sure the sign includes essential information such as contact details and the availability of brochures or flyers. Choose a professional design and ensure the text is clear and easy to read from a distance.

2. **Directional Signs:** Use directional signs strategically to guide potential buyers to your property, especially if it's located in a complex or hard-to-find area. Place signs at key intersections or street corners, leading buyers directly to your home. Make sure the signs are clear, concise, and compliant with local regulations.

3. **Well-Designed Flyers:** Create visually appealing flyers that highlight the key features and selling points of your home. Include high-quality photos, relevant details, and contact information. Use a professional layout and consider hiring a graphic designer to ensure a polished appearance. Print the flyers in sufficient quantities to distribute them at open houses, local businesses, and community bulletin boards.

4. **Effective Content:** Craft compelling and concise content for your flyers. Emphasize the unique features, location advantages, recent renovations, and any special amenities your home offers. Use descriptive language that captures buyers' attention and piques their interest. Highlight the value proposition of your property and explain how it meets the needs and desires of potential buyers.

5. **Clear Contact Information:** Make sure your contact information is prominently displayed on both the signage and flyers. Include your name, phone number, email address, and any relevant website or social media links. Potential buyers should easily find a way to reach out to you for more information or to schedule a showing.

6. **Distribution Channels:** Place flyers in prominent locations where potential buyers are likely to see them. Consider local businesses, community centers, libraries, coffee shops, and grocery stores. Seek permission from the establishment to display your flyers in high-traffic areas. Distribute them at community events, networking functions, and open houses. Additionally, provide a stack of flyers for interested visitors to take with them after viewing your property.

7. **Online Versions:** Convert your flyer into a digital format for online distribution. Create a downloadable PDF version of the flyer that can be easily shared via email or uploaded to real estate websites and social media platforms. Online versions allow interested parties to

save and share the information digitally, expanding the reach of your marketing efforts.

8. **Call-to-Action:** Include a strong call-to-action on your flyers, prompting potential buyers to take the next step. This could be an invitation to attend an open house, schedule a private showing, or contact you for more details. Encourage them to act quickly by emphasizing the limited availability or special features of your home.

9. **Consistent Branding:** Maintain consistent branding across all your marketing materials, including signage and flyers. Use the same color schemes, fonts, and logo to create a cohesive and professional image. Consistent branding helps potential buyers recognize your listings and builds credibility.

10. **Monitor and Replace:** Regularly monitor the condition of your signage and flyers. Replace any weathered or damaged signs promptly, as they can create a negative impression. Keep an ample supply of fresh flyers to ensure availability at all times.

Signage and flyers are part of a comprehensive marketing strategy. They should be used in conjunction with other marketing channels, such as online platforms and real estate agents, to maximize exposure for your home. By employing effective signage and distributing compelling flyers, you increase the visibility of your listing and attract potential buyers to learn more about your property.

CREATING A BUZZ THROUGH MEDIA AND PRESS COVERAGE

Creating a buzz through media and press coverage can significantly enhance the visibility of your home listing and attract potential buyers. Here's how you can generate media interest and leverage press coverage when selling your home:

1. **Write a Compelling Press Release:** Craft a well-written press release that highlights the unique features, selling points, and key details of your home. Include information about recent renovations, noteworthy architectural elements, or any interesting stories related to the property. Emphasize what sets your home apart from others in the market.

2. **Identify Media Outlets:** Research local media outlets such as newspapers, magazines, television stations, and online publications that cover real estate, lifestyle, or local interest stories. Make a list of relevant journalists or reporters who specialize in real estate or home-related topics.

3. **Pitch the Story:** Reach out to journalists and reporters with a personalized pitch, explaining why your home is newsworthy and would interest their audience. Highlight any unique aspects, historical significance, or notable

features of the property. Offer them the opportunity to visit the home for a personal tour or interview.

4. **Provide Visuals:** Include high-quality photos of your home in the press release or offer them separately to media outlets. Professional photographs can greatly enhance the visual appeal and make your home more enticing to potential buyers. Consider hiring a real estate photographer who specializes in capturing the essence and beauty of properties.

5. **Offer Exclusive Opportunities:** Provide exclusive access or opportunities to media outlets to increase their interest in covering your home. Offer exclusive interviews, behind-the-scenes tours, or the chance to showcase the home's unique features. This can create a sense of exclusivity and increase the chances of media coverage.

6. **Host Media Open Houses:** Organize dedicated media open houses or tours for journalists and reporters. This allows them to experience the home firsthand and gather material for their stories. Provide them with additional information, press kits, or property fact sheets during the visit.

7. **Collaborate with Real Estate Agents:** Work closely with your real estate agent to leverage their existing relationships with local media outlets. Experienced agents often have connections and can help facilitate media coverage. Share your press release and media pitch with your agent, and collaborate on strategies to generate buzz through press coverage.

8. **Share the Story on Social Media:** Utilize your social media platforms to share the media coverage of your home. Post links to articles, interviews, or features about your property. Encourage your network to share the news with their connections, widening the reach of the coverage.

9. **Monitor and Respond:** Keep track of media coverage and monitor any online comments or discussions related to your home. Respond promptly to inquiries or comments from interested parties. Engaging with potential buyers or individuals who have seen the coverage can create further interest and generate leads.

10. **Follow-Up and Express Gratitude:** Express your gratitude to journalists, reporters, and media outlets that provide coverage for your home. Send personalized thank-you notes or emails to show appreciation for their efforts. Building positive relationships with the media can lead to future opportunities and referrals.

■■

Of course, media coverage is not guaranteed, and it may take time to generate interest from journalists. However, by presenting your home as a unique and newsworthy property, providing engaging visuals, and collaborating with media outlets, you increase the likelihood of creating a buzz and attracting potential buyers who may have been unaware of your listing.

CHAPTER 7
NEGOTIATING OFFERS AND CLOSING THE DEAL

HANDLING OFFERS AND MULTIPLE OFFERS

Handling offers, especially multiple offers, when selling your home requires careful consideration and effective negotiation skills. Here's a step-by-step guide on how to handle offers and multiple offers:

1. **Review Each Offer:** Carefully review each offer received. Consider the offered price, contingencies, proposed closing date, financing terms, and any additional terms or conditions. Evaluate the overall strength of each offer and its alignment with your selling goals.

2. **Communicate with Buyers:** Reach out to each buyer's agent to acknowledge receipt of the offer and express appreciation for their interest. Request any clarifications

or additional information that may be necessary for your evaluation.

3. **Set a Deadline:** Set a deadline for all interested buyers to submit their best and final offers. This allows you to compare offers and make an informed decision. Clearly communicate the deadline to the buyers and their agents to create a sense of urgency.

4. **Consider Multiple Offers:** If you receive multiple offers, carefully compare them side by side. Evaluate the financial strength of each buyer, including their down payment amount, pre-approval status, and the likelihood of obtaining financing. Assess any contingencies or special requests within each offer.

5. **Evaluate Terms and Conditions:** Consider not only the price but also the terms and conditions of each offer. Assess the proposed closing date, contingencies (such as inspection or appraisal contingencies), and any additional requests made by the buyer. Determine which offer aligns best with your desired timeline and minimizes potential risks.

6. **Counteroffer or Accept:** Based on your evaluation, you have two options: counteroffer or accept an offer. If none of the offers meet your expectations, you can counteroffer to one or more buyers, outlining the terms you find favorable. If an offer meets your requirements, you can choose to accept it.

7. **Communicate Clearly:** Clearly communicate your decision to all parties involved. Promptly notify the

buyer's agent of your acceptance or counteroffer. Be transparent and maintain open lines of communication throughout the negotiation process to build trust and avoid misunderstandings.

8. **Respond to Counteroffers:** If you receive counteroffers from buyers, carefully evaluate them. Consider the proposed changes and how they align with your selling goals. Negotiate counteroffers based on your priorities and be prepared to provide explanations or justifications for your requests.

9. **Keep Other Buyers Informed:** Keep other interested buyers informed of your decision-making process, particularly if you're in the middle of negotiations. This helps maintain their interest and provides transparency in case the accepted offer falls through.

10. **Respect Confidentiality:** Treat all offers and negotiations with confidentiality and professionalism. Avoid discussing specific details of offers with other buyers or their agents to maintain a fair and ethical process.

11. **Backup Offers:** If you receive strong backup offers, evaluate them carefully. Backup offers can provide security in case the accepted offer falls through. Keep communication open with backup buyers and their agents, ensuring they understand their position in the transaction.

12. **Consult with Your Real Estate Agent:** Throughout the offer evaluation and negotiation process, consult with

your real estate agent. They can provide valuable insights, guidance, and expertise to help you make informed decisions and navigate the negotiation process effectively.

■■

The ultimate goal is to secure the best offer that aligns with your selling goals. Carefully evaluate each offer, communicate effectively, and negotiate in good faith. A skilled real estate agent can be instrumental in guiding you through this process and maximizing the outcome.

COUNTEROFFERS AND NEGOTIATION STRATEGIES

When selling your home, counteroffers and negotiation strategies play a crucial role in reaching mutually beneficial agreements with potential buyers. Here are some tips for dealing with counteroffers and implementing effective negotiation strategies:

1. **Understand the Buyer's Perspective:** Put yourself in the buyer's shoes and try to understand their motivations, needs, and concerns. This understanding will help you tailor your counteroffer and negotiation strategy to address their interests while protecting your own.

2. **Determine Your Priorities:** Clearly identify your priorities and non-negotiable terms before entering into negotiations. This will give you a clear framework for evaluating counteroffers and making informed decisions.

3. **Respond Promptly:** Timely communication is vital during negotiations. Respond promptly to counteroffers to maintain momentum and show your seriousness in reaching a resolution.

4. **Counteroffer with Justification:** When making a counteroffer, provide a clear and concise justification for your requested changes. Highlight the reasons behind your counteroffer, such as market conditions, home improvements, or comparable sales data. Justifying your position helps the buyer understand your perspective and increases the likelihood of a successful negotiation.

5. **Negotiate More Than Price:** While price is a significant factor, remember that other terms and conditions are negotiable as well. Consider negotiating contingencies, closing dates, repairs, or other relevant terms to find common ground with the buyer.

6. **Maintain Professionalism:** Keep negotiations professional and respectful. Avoid personal attacks or emotional responses, as they can hinder the negotiation process and damage relationships. Focus on the facts, stay composed, and work towards finding mutually beneficial solutions.

7. **Explore Creative Solutions:** If a buyer's counteroffer doesn't meet your expectations, consider exploring alternative solutions. Look for creative ways to bridge the gap, such as offering seller concessions, adjusting the closing timeline, or providing incentives like home warranties or credits for repairs.

8. **Seek Win-Win Outcomes:** Strive for win-win outcomes where both parties feel satisfied with the agreement. Look for areas where you can compromise without sacrificing your bottom line. Remember, the negotiation

process is about finding common ground and reaching a mutually beneficial resolution.

9. **Leverage Market Conditions:** Stay informed about current market conditions and trends. Use this knowledge to support your negotiation position. If it's a seller's market with high demand, you may have more leverage. In a buyer's market with more inventory, flexibility may be required to secure a successful sale.

10. **Utilize a Skilled Real Estate Agent:** Enlist the expertise of a skilled real estate agent who is experienced in negotiations. A professional agent can provide valuable insights, handle communication, and negotiate on your behalf to help achieve the best possible outcome.

11. **Consider Multiple Offers:** If you receive multiple offers, leverage the competitive environment to your advantage. Engage in strategic negotiations, allowing potential buyers to improve their offers in response to competing offers. This can potentially lead to a higher sale price and more favorable terms.

12. **Know Your Bottom Line:** While negotiation is important, it's crucial to know your bottom line and be prepared to walk away if an agreement cannot be reached that aligns with your priorities and goals. Understanding your limits helps you make informed decisions and protect your interests.

■■

Successful negotiations require flexibility, effective communication, and a focus on reaching mutually beneficial agreements. By implementing these strategies and seeking professional guidance, you can navigate counteroffers and negotiations with confidence when selling your home.

MANAGING CONTINGENCIES AND INSPECTIONS

Managing contingencies and inspections when selling your home is an essential part of the process. Here are some tips to help you effectively handle contingencies and inspections:

1. **Understand the Contingencies:** Familiarize yourself with the contingencies included in the buyer's offer. Common contingencies may involve home inspections, financing, appraisal, and the sale of the buyer's current home. Review each contingency carefully to understand the specific requirements and timelines associated with them.

2. **Respond Promptly:** Once the buyer's contingencies are in place, respond promptly and adhere to the agreed-upon timelines. Timely communication and action demonstrate your commitment to the transaction and help maintain a positive rapport with the buyer.

3. **Schedule Inspections:** Coordinate with the buyer's agent to schedule inspections within the specified timeframe. This includes home inspections, termite inspections, and any other inspections requested by the buyer. Ensure that the property is accessible and in a suitable condition for the inspections.

4. **Prepare for Inspections:** Take proactive steps to prepare your home for inspections. Clean and declutter the property, make necessary repairs, and ensure that all systems and utilities are functioning properly. Clear access to key areas of the home, such as the attic, basement, and mechanical systems, to facilitate thorough inspections.

5. **Attend the Inspections:** While not required, it is generally beneficial for sellers to be present during inspections. This allows you to address any questions or concerns the inspector may have and provide necessary information about the property. However, it's essential to maintain a respectful distance and allow the inspector to perform their work without interference.

6. **Address Inspection Findings:** After the inspections, you will receive a report outlining any issues or concerns identified. Review the report carefully and consult with your real estate agent to understand the significance of the findings. Determine which repairs or remedies, if any, you are willing to address. Prioritize repairs that may affect the safety, functionality, or legal compliance of the property.

7. **Negotiate Repair Requests:** If the buyer requests repairs or remedies based on the inspection findings, carefully evaluate the requests. Consult with your real estate agent to assess the reasonableness of the requests and negotiate a mutually acceptable resolution. Consider the cost and feasibility of the repairs, as well as their potential impact on the sale.

8. **Provide Required Documentation:** If there are contingencies related to the buyer's financing or appraisal, cooperate with their requests for documentation or access to the property. Promptly provide any necessary paperwork, such as HOA documents, property disclosures, or maintenance records.

9. **Monitor Contingency Timelines:** Stay informed about the timelines associated with the buyer's contingencies. Ensure that you meet any deadlines for actions or responses required from your end. Stay in regular communication with the buyer's agent to address any concerns or questions that may arise during this period.

10. **Close Contingencies:** Once the buyer's contingencies have been satisfied or waived, you will move closer to the closing process. Work with your real estate agent, the buyer's agent, and any relevant professionals to ensure a smooth transition to the closing stage.

11. **Maintain Documentation:** Keep copies of all correspondence, agreements, inspection reports, and repair receipts for your records. These documents may be valuable for future reference or if any disputes arise.

■■

Navigating contingencies and inspections requires effective communication, collaboration, and a willingness to address issues that may arise. Working closely with your real estate agent and staying proactive throughout the process will help ensure a successful and seamless transaction.

THE IMPORTANCE OF TIMELY COMMUNICATION

Timely communication is of utmost importance when selling your home. It plays a vital role in maintaining a smooth and successful transaction. Here are the reasons why timely communication is crucial:

1. **Building Trust:** Prompt and consistent communication helps build trust between you, the seller, and potential buyers. Timely responses to inquiries, offers, and requests demonstrate your commitment and professionalism. This trust can positively influence the buyer's perception of you as a reliable and motivated seller.

2. **Maintaining Interest:** In a competitive real estate market, there are often multiple interested buyers. Timely communication keeps potential buyers engaged and interested in your property. Delayed responses or lack of communication may lead to frustration and cause interested buyers to lose interest or turn their attention to other listings.

3. **Negotiation Efficiency:** Effective negotiations require quick and efficient communication. Delayed responses can hinder the negotiation process, lead to misunderstandings, or cause offers to expire. Timely communication allows you to respond promptly to

counteroffers, provide requested information, and keep negotiations progressing smoothly.

4. **Mitigating Issues:** Real estate transactions involve various parties, including buyers, agents, lenders, and inspectors. Timely communication helps address any issues or concerns that may arise during the selling process. By promptly addressing and resolving these issues, you can minimize their impact on the transaction and maintain a positive momentum.

5. **Meeting Deadlines:** Timely communication ensures that you meet important deadlines throughout the selling process. This includes responding to offers within specified timeframes, providing requested documents, scheduling inspections, and adhering to contractual obligations. Failing to meet these deadlines due to delayed communication can lead to complications and potential legal consequences.

6. **Buyer Satisfaction:** Buyers appreciate sellers who communicate promptly and efficiently. It allows them to obtain the information they need, make informed decisions, and proceed with confidence. Positive buyer experiences contribute to smoother negotiations, higher chances of closing the sale, and potential referrals or positive reviews.

7. **Real Estate Agent Collaboration:** Timely communication with your real estate agent is essential. Your agent relies on your prompt responses to coordinate showings, provide updates, and make informed decisions. Clear and timely communication

with your agent helps them effectively represent your interests and ensure a successful selling experience.

8. **Market Dynamics:** Real estate markets can change rapidly, and timing is crucial. Timely communication allows you to capitalize on market opportunities, such as increased demand or favorable conditions. Quick responses to offers or adjustments in pricing can help you stay competitive and attract potential buyers.

■■

Selling a home is a time-sensitive process, and timely communication is key to its success. Responding promptly to inquiries, offers, and requests demonstrates your commitment, professionalism, and respect for potential buyers and the transaction as a whole. By prioritizing timely communication, you can enhance your chances of a smooth and efficient sale.

CHAPTER 8

OVERCOMING COMMON CHALLENGES

DEALING WITH LOWBALL OFFERS

Dealing with lowball offers can be challenging, but it's important to approach them with a strategic mindset. Here are some tips on how to handle lowball offers when selling your home:

1. **Stay Calm and Objective:** It's natural to feel frustrated or insulted by a lowball offer, but it's essential to stay calm and approach the situation objectively. Remember that negotiating is part of the process, and the initial offer may not reflect the buyer's final willingness to pay.

2. **Evaluate the Offer:** Carefully evaluate the details of the offer beyond just the price. Consider the terms, contingencies, and any additional factors that may impact the overall value. Assess the buyer's financial

capability, motivation, and their history of offers or transactions.

3. **Assess Market Conditions:** Analyze the current market conditions, comparable sales in the area, and recent trends. Determine whether the lowball offer is an outlier or if it aligns with the prevailing market conditions. This information will help you determine your negotiating stance.

4. **Respond Professionally:** Respond to the lowball offer in a professional and respectful manner. Avoid emotional reactions or engaging in heated exchanges. Counter the offer with a reasonable and well-justified response that reflects your desired sale price.

5. **Justify Your Counteroffer:** Provide a solid justification for your counteroffer, supporting it with market data, recent sales, or any significant improvements or features of your home. Highlight the value your property offers to differentiate it from others in the market.

6. **Consider a Middle Ground:** If the initial lowball offer is far below your expectations, you may choose to counter with a more moderate price closer to your desired range. This can demonstrate your willingness to negotiate while maintaining a reasonable position.

7. **Negotiate Terms:** If the buyer's offer price is significantly below your expectations, consider negotiating other terms instead of focusing solely on the price. This could involve adjusting closing dates,

contingencies, repairs, or other conditions that may be favorable to both parties.

8. **Seek Guidance from Your Agent:** Rely on the expertise of your real estate agent to guide you through the negotiation process. They can provide insights into the market, assist in evaluating offers, and offer strategic advice on how to handle lowball offers effectively.

9. **Be Prepared to Walk Away:** If the buyer is unwilling to move closer to your desired price or if their offers consistently fall far below your expectations, be prepared to walk away and explore other opportunities. It's important to recognize your bottom line and avoid settling for an unsatisfactory offer.

10. **Remain Open to Negotiation:** Keep the lines of communication open and remain willing to negotiate. Sometimes, lowball offers can be a starting point for a successful negotiation that leads to a mutually acceptable agreement. Maintain a professional and collaborative approach to maximize the chances of finding common ground.

The home selling process will involve some negotiation, and lowball offers may be part of that process. By staying objective, responding professionally, and being strategic in your counteroffers, you can navigate lowball offers effectively and work towards achieving a successful sale at a fair price.

HANDLING BUYER OBJECTIONS AND CONCERNS

Handling buyer objections and concerns is an important part of selling your home. Here are some strategies to effectively address and overcome objections:

1. **Listen and Understand:** When a buyer expresses an objection or concern, listen attentively and seek to understand their perspective. Let them fully articulate their thoughts and feelings without interruption. Demonstrating empathy and understanding can help build rapport and trust.

2. **Remain Calm and Professional:** It's essential to stay calm and professional when addressing buyer objections. Responding defensively or emotionally can escalate the situation and hinder productive communication. Maintain a positive and composed demeanor throughout the discussion.

3. **Address Concerns with Information:** Provide factual and relevant information to address the buyer's concerns. Back up your responses with data, documentation, or professional opinions, if necessary. By presenting accurate information, you can help alleviate doubts and provide reassurance.

4. **Offer Solutions:** Instead of dismissing objections outright, focus on finding solutions that address the buyer's concerns. Collaborate with the buyer to explore alternatives or compromises that can meet both parties' needs. This proactive approach demonstrates your willingness to work towards a mutually beneficial outcome.

5. **Highlight the Home's Benefits:** Emphasize the unique features, benefits, and positive aspects of your home. Draw attention to its strengths and how it fulfills the buyer's requirements. Help the buyer envision themselves living in the home by showcasing its potential and value.

6. **Provide Additional Documentation or Inspections:** If a buyer has specific concerns, offer to provide additional documentation or inspections to address those concerns. For example, providing a recent home inspection report, warranty information, or maintenance records can help alleviate doubts about the home's condition.

7. **Offer a Home Warranty:** Consider offering a home warranty as an added incentive. A home warranty can provide buyers with peace of mind, as it covers certain repairs or replacements of major systems or appliances after the sale. This can help address concerns about potential future costs.

8. **Be Flexible and Accommodating:** When feasible, be willing to accommodate reasonable requests or preferences from the buyer. This could include adjusting

the closing date, offering a credit for repairs, or including certain items in the sale. Flexibility demonstrates your commitment to reaching a mutually satisfactory agreement.

9. **Engage with Your Real Estate Agent:** Leverage the expertise of your real estate agent to help address buyer objections. Your agent can provide guidance, offer insights into common objections, and propose effective strategies for overcoming them.

10. **Maintain Open Lines of Communication:** Communication is key in addressing buyer objections. Maintain open and responsive communication channels with the buyer and their agent. Promptly address any questions or concerns that arise throughout the process.

11. **Stay Positive and Patient:** Selling a home can be a complex process, and objections are a normal part of it. Stay positive and patient as you navigate through objections and work towards a resolution. A positive attitude can help maintain a constructive atmosphere and increase the chances of finding common ground.

■■

Every buyer is unique, and their objections may vary. By actively listening, providing information, offering solutions, and collaborating with the buyer, you can address their concerns effectively and increase the likelihood of a successful sale.

NAVIGATING THROUGH FINANCING AND APPRAISAL HURDLES

Navigating financial and appraisal hurdles when selling your home requires careful attention and proactive measures. Here are some strategies to help you navigate these challenges:

1. **Understand the Financial Hurdles:** Familiarize yourself with common financial hurdles that can arise during the selling process. These may include buyer financing issues, low appraisals, or challenges with loan approvals. Understanding these potential hurdles allows you to be better prepared to address them.

2. **Set Realistic Expectations:** Be aware that financial and appraisal hurdles are not uncommon in real estate transactions. Setting realistic expectations from the outset can help you navigate these challenges with patience and a proactive mindset.

3. **Work with a Knowledgeable Real Estate Agent:** Enlist the help of an experienced real estate agent who can guide you through the complexities of financial and appraisal hurdles. They have the expertise to assess potential issues early on, provide advice, and offer strategies to address them effectively.

4. **Price Your Home Appropriately:** Pricing your home appropriately from the start can help minimize the risk of financial and appraisal challenges. An overpriced home may struggle to attract qualified buyers or receive favorable appraisals. Collaborate with your real estate agent to determine a competitive and realistic listing price based on market conditions and comparable sales.

5. **Encourage Pre-Approval for Buyers:** Encouraging potential buyers to obtain pre-approval for financing can help minimize the risk of financing issues down the line. Pre-approval indicates that the buyer has undergone a preliminary evaluation of their financial situation and is more likely to secure a loan successfully.

6. **Prepare the Home for Appraisal:** Take proactive steps to prepare your home for the appraisal process. Clean and declutter the property, address any maintenance issues, and highlight its desirable features. Provide the appraiser with information on recent renovations, upgrades, or improvements that may positively impact the appraisal value.

7. **Be Present for the Appraisal:** If possible, be present during the appraisal to answer any questions the appraiser may have about the property. This allows you to provide valuable insights and share information that may positively influence the appraisal outcome.

8. **Obtain a Second Opinion:** If you receive a low appraisal that you believe does not reflect the true value of your home, you may consider obtaining a second

opinion. Consult with your real estate agent to explore the possibility of challenging the appraisal and providing additional evidence to support your case.

9. **Be Flexible in Negotiations:** In the face of financial and appraisal challenges, be open to negotiation and finding solutions that work for both parties. This could involve adjusting the sale price, offering concessions, or exploring alternative financing options. Flexibility and willingness to find common ground can help overcome hurdles.

10. **Seek Professional Advice:** Consult with professionals such as real estate attorneys, mortgage brokers, or appraisers, if necessary, to obtain expert advice on specific financial or appraisal hurdles. Their insights can help you understand the options available and make informed decisions.

■■

Financial and appraisal hurdles are common in real estate transactions. By being proactive, working closely with your real estate agent, and seeking professional advice when needed, you can navigate these challenges effectively and increase the likelihood of a successful sale.

TIME-SENSITIVE ISSUES AND CONTINGENCIES

Handling time-sensitive issues and contingencies when selling your home requires a proactive and organized approach. Here are some strategies to effectively manage these situations:

1. **Understand the Contingencies:** Familiarize yourself with the contingencies involved in the sale process, such as financing, home inspections, appraisal, and buyer's sale of their own property. Each contingency has a specific timeline and requirements that must be met within a certain timeframe.

2. **Create a Timeline:** Develop a detailed timeline that outlines important milestones and deadlines related to the sale. This includes contingency periods, inspection dates, financing deadlines, and closing dates. Share this timeline with all relevant parties, including your real estate agent, the buyer, and any involved professionals.

3. **Communicate Expectations:** Clearly communicate your expectations regarding timelines and contingencies to all parties involved. Make sure everyone is aware of the necessary actions and the importance of meeting deadlines. Promptly respond to inquiries and requests for information to keep the process moving smoothly.

4. **Stay Organized:** Maintain organized records of all documentation, contracts, and correspondence related to the sale. Keep track of important dates, agreements, and any changes or amendments to the contract. This will help you stay on top of time-sensitive issues and ensure that all requirements are met within the designated timeframes.

5. **Coordinate with Your Real Estate Agent:** Work closely with your real estate agent to manage time-sensitive issues and contingencies effectively. Your agent can help monitor deadlines, facilitate communication with the buyer's agent, and ensure that necessary actions are taken within the appropriate timeframes.

6. **Promptly Respond to Requests:** Time-sensitive issues often require quick responses. Be diligent in responding to requests for documentation, information, or actions related to contingencies. Delayed responses can lead to delays in the process or even potential contract breaches.

7. **Seek Professional Assistance:** If you encounter challenges or complexities related to time-sensitive issues or contingencies, seek professional assistance. This may involve consulting with a real estate attorney, a mortgage broker, a home inspector, or other relevant professionals who can provide guidance and help you navigate the situation effectively.

8. **Flexibility and Problem-Solving:** Be prepared for unexpected situations and be willing to adapt and problem-solve as needed. This may involve adjusting

timelines, negotiating with the buyer, or finding alternative solutions to meet the requirements of contingencies.

9. **Maintain Open Lines of Communication:** Effective communication is crucial when dealing with time-sensitive issues and contingencies. Keep all parties informed of any changes, updates, or progress related to contingencies. Regularly communicate with the buyer's agent, professionals involved, and your real estate agent to ensure everyone is on the same page.

10. **Focus on Resolution:** Approach time-sensitive issues and contingencies with a problem-solving mindset. Instead of dwelling on setbacks or challenges, focus on finding solutions and moving the process forward. Collaborate with all parties involved to address any issues that arise and work towards a successful resolution.

■■

Remember to stay organized, communicate effectively, and take proactive measures, so that you can effectively handle time-sensitive issues and contingencies during the home-selling process.

CHAPTER 9

WORKING WITH PROFESSIONALS

CHOOSING THE RIGHT REAL ESTATE AGENT

Choosing the right real estate agent is crucial when selling your home as they will play a significant role in the success of your sale. Here are some steps to help you choose the right real estate agent:

1. **Research Local Agents:** Start by researching local real estate agents in your area. Look for agents who have experience and a track record of success in selling homes similar to yours. Seek recommendations from friends, family, or neighbors who have recently sold their homes.

2. **Read Reviews and Testimonials:** Look for online reviews and testimonials from previous clients of the agents you are considering. Pay attention to the feedback regarding their communication skills, negotiation abilities, market knowledge, and overall professionalism.

3. **Interview Multiple Agents:** Schedule interviews or consultations with at least three potential agents. Prepare a list of questions to ask them, focusing on their experience, marketing strategies, track record, and their knowledge of your local market. Take note of their responses and assess their compatibility with your needs and expectations.

4. **Evaluate Experience and Expertise:** Consider the experience and expertise of each agent. Look for an agent who specializes in selling homes in your price range and neighborhood. Ask about their marketing strategies, negotiation skills, and their understanding of current market trends.

5. **Assess Communication and Responsiveness:** Communication is key in a successful real estate transaction. Assess how well the agents communicate and respond to your inquiries during the initial interview process. A responsive and attentive agent will be proactive in keeping you updated and addressing your concerns throughout the selling process.

6. **Request a Comparative Market Analysis (CMA):** Ask each agent to provide you with a comparative market analysis (CMA) for your home. The CMA will give you an estimate of your home's value based on recent comparable sales in your area. Compare the CMAs provided by different agents to assess their accuracy and knowledge of the local market.

7. **Consider Marketing Strategies:** Inquire about the agents' marketing strategies for selling your home. Look

for agents who utilize a comprehensive and tailored approach to marketing, including online listings, professional photography, virtual tours, and social media promotion. Ask for examples of their previous marketing campaigns.

8. **Check Licensing and Credentials:** Ensure that the agents you are considering are licensed and registered with the appropriate regulatory bodies in your region. You can typically verify their credentials through your local real estate licensing authority.

9. **Request References:** Ask potential agents for references from previous clients. Contact these clients to inquire about their experience working with the agent, their satisfaction with the service provided, and the overall outcome of their home sale.

10. **Trust Your Instincts:** Ultimately, trust your instincts when choosing a real estate agent. Consider the level of rapport, professionalism, and trustworthiness you feel when interacting with each agent. Select an agent with whom you feel comfortable and confident in their ability to represent your best interests.

■■

Selling a home is a significant transaction, so take the time to select a real estate agent who is experienced, knowledgeable, and aligned with your goals. A reliable agent can guide you through the selling process, provide valuable insights, and help you achieve a successful sale.

COLLABORATING WITH HOME STAGING PROFESSIONALS

Collaborating with home staging professionals can greatly enhance the marketability and appeal of your home when selling. Here's how to effectively work with home staging professionals:

1. **Research and Select a Reputable Home Stager:** Begin by researching and selecting a reputable home staging professional in your area. Look for stagers with a proven track record, positive reviews, and a portfolio of successfully staged properties. Seek recommendations from your real estate agent or other homeowners who have previously used staging services.

2. **Schedule an Initial Consultation:** Contact the home staging professional to schedule an initial consultation. During this meeting, the stager will assess your home's current condition, discuss your goals, and provide recommendations for staging based on the target market and potential buyers.

3. **Establish Open Communication:** Maintain open and clear communication with the home stager throughout the staging process. Share important information about your home, including its unique features, any existing challenges, or specific areas of concern. Collaborate

with the stager to ensure their vision aligns with your goals and expectations.

4. **Discuss Budget and Timeline:** Discuss your budget and desired timeline with the home stager upfront. They can provide guidance on how to best allocate your budget to maximize the impact of the staging. Establish a timeline for completing the staging process, taking into account any upcoming photography sessions, open houses, or buyer showings.

5. **Remove Personal Items and Declutter:** Prepare your home for staging by removing personal items and decluttering each room. This will allow the stager to showcase the home's features effectively and create a clean, spacious, and inviting environment. Consider storing personal belongings off-site or renting a temporary storage unit if necessary.

6. **Trust the Stager's Expertise:** Remember that home staging professionals are trained to create an appealing and marketable space. Trust their expertise and creative vision when it comes to furniture arrangement, decor selection, and overall design choices. Be open to their suggestions and ideas, even if they differ from your personal style.

7. **Discuss Furniture and Accessory Rental:** If your home needs additional furniture or accessories for staging, discuss rental options with the stager. They can recommend suitable rental companies or handle the rental process on your behalf. Ensure that the rental

items complement the style and size of your home, enhancing its overall appeal.

8. **Prepare for Showings and Photography:** Work closely with the home stager to prepare your home for showings and photography. They will guide you on how to maintain the staged look, including tips on furniture placement, lighting, and cleanliness. Follow their advice to present your home in its best possible condition to potential buyers.

9. **Maintain Communication During the Selling Process:** Stay in touch with the home stager during the selling process. Provide updates on the status of your home, any changes in showing schedules, or feedback received from potential buyers. This ongoing collaboration will help the stager make necessary adjustments or recommendations to maximize the impact of the staging.

10. **Evaluate the Results:** After your home is sold, evaluate the impact of the staging on the selling process and final sale price. Reflect on the benefits of working with a home staging professional and consider sharing your positive experience with others who may be considering staging their homes.

■■

By collaborating closely with a home staging professional, you can leverage their expertise to create a visually appealing and marketable space that captures the attention of potential buyers. Together, you can enhance the overall presentation of your home and increase its chances of selling quickly and at a desirable price.

PARTNERING WITH MORTGAGE BROKERS AND LENDERS

Partnering with mortgage brokers and lenders when selling your home can be beneficial in attracting potential buyers and facilitating the financing process. Here's how to effectively collaborate with them:

1. **Research and Select Reputable Mortgage Professionals:** Research and identify reputable mortgage brokers and lenders in your area. Look for professionals with a strong track record, positive reviews, and a reputation for providing excellent customer service. Seek recommendations from your real estate agent or other homeowners who have recently sold their homes.

2. **Establish Relationships:** Reach out to mortgage brokers and lenders to introduce yourself and establish relationships. Attend networking events or schedule meetings to discuss your home-selling goals and explore opportunities for collaboration. Building personal connections with mortgage professionals can lead to valuable referrals and assistance in the selling process.

3. **Provide Information on Your Home:** Share essential information about your home with mortgage professionals, such as its features, location, selling

price, and any unique selling points. This will help them understand the property and its potential appeal to buyers seeking financing.

4. **Offer to Provide Marketing Materials:** Provide mortgage brokers and lenders with marketing materials about your home, such as high-quality photos, detailed property descriptions, and any other relevant information. This will enable them to showcase your home to their clients who may be in the market for a new property.

5. **Facilitate Communication:** Maintain open lines of communication between the buyer's mortgage professional and your real estate agent. Encourage regular updates on the progress of the buyer's financing application, any potential issues, and the overall timeline. Promptly respond to any requests for information or documentation to ensure a smooth and efficient process.

6. **Provide Access for Appraisal and Inspections:** Coordinate with the buyer's mortgage professional to provide access to your home for necessary appraisals and inspections. These are critical steps in the financing process, and timely cooperation will help expedite the transaction.

7. **Understand Financing Contingencies:** Familiarize yourself with the financing contingencies outlined in the purchase agreement. These contingencies typically specify the timeframe for the buyer to secure financing and any requirements or conditions related to the loan.

Stay informed about key dates and ensure that the buyer is meeting their obligations within the specified timeframe.

8. **Assist with Required Documentation:** Be prepared to provide any necessary documentation requested by the buyer's mortgage professional. This may include information about your home's history, repairs or renovations, and any other relevant financial or legal documents. Timely and accurate provision of documentation can help avoid delays in the financing process.

9. **Coordinate Closing Procedures:** Work with your real estate agent and the buyer's mortgage professional to coordinate the closing procedures. This includes ensuring that all necessary documentation is prepared and available, scheduling the closing date, and addressing any final requirements from the buyer's lender.

■■

Partnering with mortgage brokers and lenders will allow you to streamline the financing process for potential buyers and increase the likelihood of a successful sale. Collaborating effectively with these professionals will help create a seamless and efficient experience for both you and the buyer, ultimately leading to a smoother closing process.

ENGAGING WITH REAL ESTATE ATTORNEYS OR ESCROW AGENTS

Engaging with real estate attorneys or escrow agents when selling your home is important to ensure a smooth and legally compliant transaction. Here are the key reasons why their involvement is essential:

1. **Legal Protection:** Real estate transactions involve complex legal documents and regulations. Working with a real estate attorney or escrow agent helps protect your interests and ensures that all legal requirements are met throughout the selling process. They can review contracts, disclosure forms, and other legal documents to ensure they comply with local laws and regulations.

2. **Contract Preparation and Review:** Selling a home typically involves drafting or reviewing a purchase agreement, which is a legally binding contract. Real estate attorneys can assist in preparing or reviewing the contract to ensure that your rights and obligations are properly addressed. They can help clarify terms, negotiate contingencies, and include necessary protections specific to your situation.

3. **Title Search and Clearance:** Before selling your home, it's crucial to establish a clear title, meaning that there are no outstanding liens, encumbrances, or legal issues that could hinder the transfer of ownership. Real estate

attorneys or escrow agents can conduct a thorough title search to identify any potential issues and help resolve them, ensuring a clean title for the buyer.

4. **Escrow Services:** Escrow agents play a vital role in the closing process. They act as neutral third parties and hold funds and documents in escrow until all conditions of the sale are met. This includes verifying that necessary inspections, repairs, and other contingencies have been fulfilled before releasing funds to the appropriate parties. Escrow agents facilitate the secure transfer of funds and documents, providing protection for both the buyer and seller.

5. **Legal Advice and Guidance:** Real estate attorneys can provide invaluable legal advice and guidance throughout the selling process. They can help navigate complex legal issues, answer any questions or concerns you may have, and provide strategic advice on negotiation, disclosures, and potential risks. Their expertise ensures that you make informed decisions that align with your best interests.

6. **Mitigating Disputes:** Selling a home can sometimes lead to disputes or disagreements between the buyer and seller. Having a real estate attorney or escrow agent involved can help mitigate potential conflicts by providing objective advice and guidance. They can mediate disputes and help find fair resolutions, potentially saving you time, stress, and costly legal battles.

7. **Compliance with Local Regulations:** Real estate transactions are subject to various local, state, and federal regulations. Real estate attorneys or escrow agents are familiar with these regulations and can ensure that you comply with all legal requirements throughout the selling process. This includes adhering to disclosure obligations, fair housing laws, and any other applicable regulations.

8. **Closing Procedures and Documentation:** Real estate attorneys or escrow agents facilitate the closing procedures and ensure that all necessary documentation is properly prepared and executed. They oversee the transfer of funds, coordinate with lenders, review closing statements, and address any last-minute issues that may arise. Their involvement helps ensure a smooth and efficient closing process.

∎∎

While working with a real estate attorney or escrow agent may involve additional costs, their expertise and legal guidance can provide invaluable protection and peace of mind throughout the selling process. Consider consulting with professionals in your area to understand how they can best support you in your specific circumstances.

CHAPTER 10

POST-SALE CONSIDERATIONS

MOVING AND RELOCATION TIPS

Moving and relocating can be a significant undertaking when selling your home. Here are some tips to help you navigate the process smoothly:

1. **Plan Ahead:** Start planning your move as soon as you decide to sell your home. Create a timeline and checklist of tasks to be completed before, during, and after the sale. This will help you stay organized and ensure that everything is in order for a seamless transition.

2. **Declutter and Organize:** Take the opportunity to declutter your belongings before you move. Sort through your items and decide what to keep, donate, sell, or discard. This will not only reduce the amount of stuff you have to move but also make your home more appealing to potential buyers.

3. **Hire Professional Movers:** Consider hiring professional movers to handle the packing, loading, and transportation of your belongings. Research and obtain quotes from reputable moving companies to ensure you choose one that fits your budget and requirements. Read reviews and ask for recommendations from friends or your real estate agent.

4. **Obtain Multiple Moving Quotes:** If you decide to hire professional movers, it's advisable to obtain multiple quotes from different companies. Compare their services, prices, insurance coverage, and customer reviews to make an informed decision. Ensure that the moving company is licensed and insured to protect your belongings during the relocation process.

5. **Notify Service Providers and Change Address:** Notify your service providers, such as utility companies, internet and cable providers, banks, insurance companies, and any other relevant institutions, about your upcoming move. Arrange for the transfer or cancellation of services and update your address with them. Also, update your address with the postal service and notify friends, family, and important contacts of your new address.

6. **Pack Efficiently:** Start packing well in advance, beginning with items you rarely use or seasonal belongings. Use sturdy boxes, packing materials, and labeling systems to keep track of your belongings. Pack similar items together and label each box with its contents and the room it belongs to. This will make

unpacking and organizing at your new home much easier.

7. **Coordinate Closing Dates:** If you're simultaneously buying a new home, coordinate the closing dates of your current and new homes to minimize the time gap between moving out and moving in. This will help avoid the need for temporary housing or storage solutions. Work closely with your real estate agent, lenders, and any other parties involved to ensure a smooth transition.

8. **Arrange for Storage, if Needed:** If there's a time gap between selling your current home and moving into your new one, consider arranging for temporary storage for your belongings. Research storage facilities in your area and book in advance to secure the desired space. Take an inventory of the items you're storing and consider obtaining insurance for the stored items.

9. **Update Home Security**: Before you move out of your current home, update the security measures. Change the locks or consider rekeying them to ensure that only authorized individuals can access your property. Inform your security system provider about your move and discuss any necessary changes or transfers of service.

10. **Take Care of Personal Documents:** Keep important documents, such as passports, birth certificates, insurance policies, and financial records, in a safe and easily accessible place during the move. Consider carrying them with you personally rather than packing them with the rest of your belongings to ensure their security.

11. **Take Care of Pets**: If you have pets, make arrangements for their care during the move. Consider boarding them or arranging for a trusted friend or family member to look after them on moving day. Ensure that their microchip information and identification tags are up to date with your new contact details.

12. **Plan for Essentials:** Pack a separate box with essential items that you'll need immediately upon arrival at your new home. This may include toiletries, a change of clothes, bedding, etc.

UNDERSTANDING TAX IMPLICATIONS AND DEDUCTIONS

Understanding the tax implications and deductions when selling your home is important to ensure compliance with tax laws and optimize your financial situation. Here are some key points to consider:

1. **Capital Gains Tax:** The sale of your primary residence may be subject to capital gains tax, depending on the profit you make from the sale. However, there are certain exemptions and deductions available that can help reduce or eliminate your tax liability.

2. **Primary Residence Exemption:** In many countries, including the United States, there is a primary residence exemption that allows homeowners to exclude a certain amount of capital gains from taxation. It is essential to understand the specific criteria and requirements for claiming this exemption in your jurisdiction.

3. **Ownership and Use Tests:** To qualify for the primary residence exemption, you typically need to have owned and used the property as your primary residence for a certain period, such as two out of the last five years before the sale. Ensure you meet these ownership and use tests to be eligible for the exemption.

4. **Married Couples Filing Jointly**: If you are married and filing jointly, the primary residence exemption may allow you to exclude a higher amount of capital gains from taxation. Be sure to understand the rules and limits for married couples to maximize your tax benefits.

5. **Consult with a Tax Professional:** Tax laws and regulations can be complex, and they vary between jurisdictions. It is advisable to consult with a qualified tax professional or accountant who specializes in real estate transactions to understand the specific tax implications and deductions relevant to your situation.

6. **Record-Keeping:** Keep thorough records of your home-related expenses and improvements over the years. This includes receipts, invoices, and documentation of any upgrades, renovations, or repairs made to the property. These records can help substantiate deductions and reduce your taxable capital gains.

7. **Deductible Expenses:** Some expenses related to selling your home may be deductible, such as real estate agent commissions, legal fees, advertising costs, and certain home improvement expenses made to facilitate the sale. Consult with a tax professional to understand the specific deductible expenses allowed in your jurisdiction.

8. **1031 Exchange:** In the United States, a 1031 exchange allows for the deferral of capital gains tax if you reinvest the proceeds from the sale of your home into a similar investment property. This can be a complex strategy,

and it is important to consult with a tax professional to understand the specific rules and requirements.

9. **State and Local Taxes:** Be aware that there may be additional state or local taxes applicable to the sale of your home. Research and understand the tax laws specific to your jurisdiction to ensure compliance and proper reporting.

10. **Non-Resident Tax Considerations:** If you are a non-resident selling a property in a different country, there may be specific tax obligations and regulations to be aware of. Consult with tax professionals in both your home country and the country where the property is located to understand the tax implications and any potential tax treaties or exemptions that may apply.

■■

Remember, tax laws are subject to change, so it is important to stay updated and consult with a qualified tax professional to ensure you are fully informed about the tax implications and deductions specific to your situation.

CLOSING DOCUMENTATION AND LEGAL OBLIGATIONS

When selling your home, there are several closing documents and legal obligations that need to be fulfilled. These requirements may vary depending on your jurisdiction, but here are some common aspects to consider:

1. **Purchase Agreement:** The purchase agreement is a legally binding contract between you and the buyer. It outlines the terms and conditions of the sale, including the purchase price, contingencies, and closing date. Ensure that the agreement is accurate, reflects your negotiations, and is reviewed by a real estate attorney if necessary.

2. **Property Disclosures:** In many jurisdictions, sellers are required to provide certain disclosures about the property's condition, known issues, and any other relevant information that may affect the buyer's decision. These disclosures help ensure transparency and protect both parties from potential disputes or legal issues.

3. **Title Search and Title Insurance**: A title search is conducted to verify the legal ownership of the property and to identify any liens, encumbrances, or legal issues

that may impact the sale. Title insurance is typically obtained to protect the buyer and lender against any future claims or disputes related to the property's title.

4. **Closing Statement or Settlement Statement:** A closing statement provides an itemized breakdown of the financial transactions related to the sale. It includes the purchase price, prorated taxes and fees, real estate agent commissions, and any other costs associated with the transaction. Both the buyer and seller review and sign this document.

5. **Transfer of Ownership:** The legal transfer of ownership, known as conveyancing, involves the preparation and execution of various documents. This typically includes a deed or transfer document that transfers ownership from you to the buyer. The deed is recorded with the appropriate government agency to establish the buyer's legal ownership of the property.

6. **Paying off Existing Loans and Liens:** If you have outstanding loans or liens on the property, these need to be addressed before closing. The proceeds from the sale are typically used to pay off any existing mortgage or liens on the property. Ensure that all necessary payments are made to clear the title and release any obligations.

7. **Prorated Expenses:** Property taxes, homeowner association fees, and other expenses may need to be prorated between you and the buyer based on the closing date. The exact calculations and responsibilities

for these prorated expenses should be outlined in the purchase agreement or negotiated separately.

8. **Government Filings and Fees:** There may be various government filings and fees required when selling your home. This can include the transfer of property records, paying transfer taxes, and updating relevant government agencies with the change in ownership. Be aware of the specific requirements in your jurisdiction and ensure compliance.

9. **Closing Costs:** As the seller, you may be responsible for certain closing costs associated with the sale. These can include real estate agent commissions, attorney fees, title insurance, and other administrative costs. Understand your financial obligations and review the closing statement to ensure accuracy.

10. **Final Walk-Through:** Before closing, the buyer typically conducts a final walk-through of the property to ensure that it is in the agreed-upon condition. This is an opportunity for the buyer to verify that any agreed-upon repairs or improvements have been completed and to confirm that the property is in the expected state.

■■

It is important to consult with a real estate attorney or work closely with a qualified real estate agent who can guide you through the specific closing documentation and legal obligations in your jurisdiction. They will help ensure that all necessary documents are prepared, reviewed, and executed correctly to facilitate a smooth and legally compliant transaction.

EVALUATING YOUR SELLING EXPERIENCE FOR FUTURE REFERENCE

Evaluating your selling experience is essential for future reference and improvement. Here are some steps you can take to assess your selling experience:

1. **Reflect on Your Goals:** Begin by reflecting on your initial goals and objectives for selling your home. Did you achieve what you set out to accomplish? Consider factors such as the timeline, sale price, and overall outcome.

2. **Review the Selling Process:** Take a comprehensive look at the selling process from start to finish. Assess each stage, including preparation, marketing, showings, negotiations, and closing. Identify both strengths and areas for improvement.

3. **Analyze the Market:** Evaluate the market conditions during your home sale. Research comparable sales, inventory levels, and any external factors that may have influenced your selling experience. This will help you understand the broader market dynamics that may have affected your results.

4. **Assess Pricing Strategy:** Review your pricing strategy and its impact on buyer interest and offers received. Consider whether the initial listing price was realistic

and competitive for the market. Evaluate any price adjustments made and their effectiveness.

5. **Consider Marketing and Exposure:** Evaluate the effectiveness of your marketing efforts in generating interest and attracting potential buyers. Assess the quality of your listing photos, the use of online platforms, social media, and other marketing channels. Determine which strategies were most successful in reaching your target audience.

6. **Reflect on Buyer Feedback:** Consider the feedback you received from potential buyers during showings and open houses. Were there recurring concerns or objections? Understanding buyer feedback can provide valuable insights into areas where your home may have fallen short or where improvements can be made.

7. **Review Agent Performance:** If you worked with a real estate agent, assess their performance. Evaluate their communication, marketing efforts, negotiation skills, and overall level of support throughout the selling process. Provide feedback to your agent, as this can help them improve their services and future transactions.

8. **Assess Transaction Documentation:** Review the accuracy and completeness of the transaction documentation, including the purchase agreement, disclosures, and closing statements. Ensure that all legal obligations were met and that you maintained thorough records of the transaction.

9. **Calculate Financial Outcomes:** Evaluate the financial outcomes of your home sale. Compare the final sale price to your initial expectations and the market value of your property. Consider the expenses incurred during the selling process, such as closing costs, repairs, and staging. Calculate your net proceeds from the sale.

10. **Identify Lessons Learned:** Based on your assessment, identify key lessons learned from your selling experience. Determine areas where you excelled and can leverage those strengths in future transactions. Also, identify areas where improvements can be made and develop strategies to address them.

11. **Seek Feedback from Others:** Consider seeking feedback from others involved in the transaction, such as the buyer's agent or professionals you worked with, like your real estate attorney or home staging professional. Their insights can provide valuable perspectives on your selling experience.

12. **Document Your Findings:** Document your findings and insights from the evaluation process. This can be in the form of notes, a summary report, or a checklist. Keep this information as a reference for future home selling endeavors.

■■

By evaluating your selling experience, you can gain valuable insights to improve future transactions, make more informed decisions, and optimize your selling strategy. Remember to apply these lessons learned in conjunction with current market conditions and seek professional advice when needed.

CHAPTER 11
CONCLUSION

Selling your home can be a complex and sometimes challenging process, but with the right approach and mindset, you can increase your chances of success. Here are some final tips and words of encouragement to help you along the way:

1. **Stay Positive:** Selling a home can be stressful, but maintaining a positive attitude throughout the process will help you stay focused and motivated. Embrace challenges as opportunities for growth and learning.

2. **Set Realistic Expectations:** Understand that selling a home takes time and may involve unexpected twists and turns. Set realistic expectations regarding the timeline, sale price, and overall outcome. Be prepared for the possibility of market fluctuations and buyer negotiations.

3. **Prepare Your Home:** Invest time and effort in preparing your home for sale. Declutter, clean, and stage your home to showcase its best features and create a welcoming environment for potential buyers. First

impressions matter, so make sure your home stands out.

4. **Price It Right:** Pricing your home appropriately is crucial. Work with a real estate professional to determine a competitive and realistic asking price based on market conditions and comparable sales. Avoid overpricing, as it can deter potential buyers, and be open to adjusting the price if needed.

5. **Market Effectively:** Develop a comprehensive marketing strategy to maximize exposure for your home. Utilize online platforms, social media, professional photography, and virtual tours to attract potential buyers. Leverage the expertise of a real estate agent to reach a wider audience.

6. **Communicate Clearly:** Maintain open and timely communication with your real estate agent, potential buyers, and other parties involved in the transaction. Respond promptly to inquiries, address concerns, and provide any requested information. Clear communication builds trust and helps keep the process on track.

7. **Be Flexible:** Be flexible with scheduling showings and open houses to accommodate potential buyers. Flexibility can increase the number of interested parties and improve your chances of receiving offers. Consider any reasonable requests for repairs or modifications from serious buyers.

8. **Negotiate Wisely:** Negotiations are a normal part of the selling process. Be prepared to negotiate on price, contingencies, and other terms. Keep your objectives in mind while being open to finding common ground that benefits both parties. Consult with your real estate agent for guidance during negotiations.
9. **Seek Professional Advice:** Enlist the support of qualified professionals such as real estate agents, attorneys, and tax advisors. Their expertise can help you navigate complex aspects of the selling process and ensure compliance with legal requirements.

10. **Stay Informed:** Stay updated on market trends, local regulations, and best practices in real estate. Knowledge is power, and being well-informed will help you make informed decisions throughout the selling process.

11. **Take Care of Yourself:** Selling a home can be demanding, both physically and emotionally. Take care of yourself by maintaining a healthy lifestyle, practicing self-care, and seeking support from friends and family. Balancing your well-being with the demands of the process is crucial.

■■

Remember, every selling experience is unique, and success may look different for each individual. Stay focused, be patient, and trust the process. With the right strategies, preparation, and support, you can successfully navigate the selling process and achieve your goals. NOW GO OUT THERE AND SELL IT LIKE IT'S HOT!

ABOUT THE AUTHOR

Tanisha Owens Barrett is a real estate agent located in Greenville, South Carolina. She has worked with several buyers, sellers, and investors over the years. Tanisha is certified in short sales and foreclosures. She is also a pricing strategy advisor, and a mentor with her current brokerage, which is eXp Realty. She is a wife and mother of one energetic 4 year old, named Noah.

Her husband is a licensed home inspector and her father-in-law is a licensed contractor. She has learned a lot during her time as a dedicated real estate professional and strives to ensure she is able to pass that information on to those around her. This book is just one avenue to do that! When she isn't spending time assisting her clients or with her family, you can likely find her on social media continuing to educate those around her.

Note from the author:

"Please buy my book. I'm a real estate agent. Sometimes I make money. Sometimes I don't."

www.ingramcontent.com/pod-product-compliance
Lightning Source LLC
Chambersburg PA
CBHW050734010526
44107CB00010B/842